Adventure is worthwhile

in itself.

AMELIA EARHART

My Travel
Journal

LONDON

D. A. MICHAELS

KPT PUBLISHING

Traveling Tips: 101

Whether you are a seasoned traveler, or taking your first adventure across the pond, we have included some of our favorite travel tips to help you have an enjoyable experience. This Journal also provides you with blank pages to jot down your travel plans and capture memories of your trip to London.

PLAN A FEW KEY POINTS OF INTEREST. Before you start, remember your days unfold naturally. Only schedule two or three things a day and let the rest happen on its own.

FLYING? BOOK A WINDOW SEAT. It's nice having a place to rest your head, especially on international flights. Seats closer to the front allow you to get to the passport line faster.

SHOP AROUND WHEN BOOKING FLIGHTS. It is often cheaper to fly into airports close to your final destination, then take trains or buses to where you are staying.

BOOK FLIGHTS 3-4 MONTHS IN ADVANCE. Advance booking will get you a better price. Also remember, spending five hours to try to save a few dollars will cause you a lot of stress.

CHECK ON VACCINATIONS. Getting sick, especially in a foreign country, is never fun and will ruin your vacation.

CARRY AN EMPTY WATER BOTTLE. Empty metal bottles will get through airport security, then simply fill it once inside. Drinking water from the tap will save money.

TRY TO USE NO-FEE BANK CARDS. Use more of your hard-earned money and spend it on your travels instead of fees.

USE POINTS AND MILES FOR DISCOUNTED TRAVEL. And remember, make sure everything you do earns you miles.

GET TRAVEL INSURANCE. If something goes wrong, you don't want to be out thousands of dollars. When traveling, it's the most important thing to get that you never hope to use.

LOOK FOR BUSINESS TRAVELERS WHEN IN SECURITY LINES. They are experienced travelers and move much faster.

MAKE COPIES OF PASSPORTS & IMPORTANT DOCUMENTS. E-mail yourself a copy so you'll almost always have access to them as a secondary backup.

EXTRA BANK & CREDIT CARDS. Unfortunate things happen and you won't want to be stuck somewhere without access to your money.

EMERGENCY CASH. Always carry some cash for the unexpected.

DON'T USE A MONEY BELT. Thieves watch for them; wearing one announces that you are a tourist.

TAKE PICTURES OF YOUR LUGGAGE AND CONTENTS. If a suitcase gets lost, photos will help identify it more easily and help in any process.

MAPS ARE YOUR FRIENDS. Looking like a tourist isn't as bad as getting really lost and ending up in the wrong neighborhood.

DON'T BE AFRAID TO WANDER A BIT. Walking without a destination is a great way to get to learn about the city better.

VISIT THE LOCAL TOURISM OFFICE. These employees are paid to know what's going on in town: free activities, special events, and they can help make your stay more event-filled.

STAY IN HOSTELS. They are less expensive, and you'll meet a lot of people! Hostel bars are also very cheap.

EARPLUGS. We all do it, but snoring may ruin a needed good night of sleep. They are small and pack anywhere.

IF YOU STAY IN A HOSTEL, ASK THE STAFF FOR INFORMATION. Even if you aren't staying in hostel, staff deal with travelers every day. They know exactly where you can go for a cheap meal and some unusual local attractions.

ALWAYS ASK FOR AN UPGRADE. When you check in to the hotel, remember they have a lot of flexibility — it never hurts to ask.

USE HOSPITALITY WEBSITES TO MEET LOCALS. Like hostel staff, they can give you a different perspective on your destination. Be open to strangers. Do, however, keep your guard up.

LEARN SOME BASIC PHRASES. Learn a few key words and phrases in the language of your travel. The people who live there will appreciate it, and it will make communicating easier.

READ ABOUT THE HISTORY OF WHERE YOU ARE GOING. You cannot understand the present without knowing about the past.

TAKE ONLY WHAT YOU NEED FOR EACH OUTING. Limit the amount of cash or cards you carry with you. In case something does happen it will make recovery easier.

BUY AN OYSTER CARD. The Oyster Card is valid not only on the underground, but also for the red double-decker buses and even regional trains. Check into this ahead of time.

ALWAYS CARRY A LOCK. Locks come in handy for protecting your valuables, especially if you are staying in a dorm.

ALWAYS BRING A JACKET. Rain comes suddenly and nights get cold.

BUY A BACKPACK OR SMALL SUITCASE. Bring half the clothes you think you'll need — you usually never wear everthing you packed anyway. Re-wearing some of your clothes is okay.

GET GOOD SHOES. You will walk. A lot. Make sure they are comfortable enough to wear all day.

PACK EXTRA SOCKS. You'll lose at least one or they all get wet, so packing a few extra might be a blessing.

PACK A FLASHLIGHT. You never know when you might need it.

ALWAYS CARRY A BASIC FIRST-AID KIT. Band-Aids, ointments, and antibacterial cream will take care of most minor scrapes.

ALWAYS CARRY A SMALL TOWEL. Not everything is planned, and you might stop at a beach, picnic, or just need to dry off.

LIKE ANYWHERE ELSE, LOOK BOTH WAYS WHEN CROSSING A STREET. This is especially important in a country whose traffic patterns are different from what you are used to.

LOOK FOR FREE WI-FI. Libraries, Starbucks, and most cafés offer free Wi-Fi connection.

VISIT HISTORICAL SITES AT LUNCHTIME — you can always eat later. Other tourists will usually go to lunch, so sites will be less crowded.

TRY THE LOCAL STREET FOOD. Never eat in the touristy areas. Walk a few blocks in either direction and you find better food, better prices. Afterall, if you don't experience the local food, you will be missing out on the culture.

SAVE EXPENSIVE RESTAURANTS FOR LUNCH. They will usually offer lunch specials — same food as dinner at half the price.

BUY SOME GROCERIES. The locals do not eat out every night — neither should you. You will save a lot of money.

RIDE ANYTHING BUT A TAXI. These are usually quite expensive.

FREE WALKING TOURS. These tours will give you a good orientation and background of the city you are in — plus save money.

CHECK OUT CITY ATTRACTION CARDS. If you plan on visiting a lot of museums or other attractions in a short period of time, a city pass is going to save you money on admission (and most provide free public transportation as well).

LEARN THE ART OF HAGGLING. Negotiating prices will help you throughout your trip, and it's often an adventure of its own.

BE RESPECTFUL. Locals are willing to help you out, but there's probably a language barrier, so keep your cool when something doesn't go your way.

BE FRUGAL, BUT NOT CHEAP. Look for deals and don't waste money, but don't miss out on great experiences or walk 10 miles to save a couple of dollars. Time is money. Spend them both wisely.

PACK AN EXTRA USB CHARGER. A charged backup battery is always a good battery.

TAKE A LOT OF PHOTOS OF AND WITH PEOPLE. Years from now, you'll want to look back on your trip and remember some of the people who made it so memorable.

WEAR SUNSCREEN. Wear something that blocks the sun even on cloudy days. Don't let sunburn ruin your trip.

Add to this list as you learn new tips, but take advantage of some tried-and-true tips from those who have traveled ahead of you. Your trip will be more enjoyable—guaranteed! The following pages are filled with journaling tips: things to help you record the memories of your dream vacation so you will be able to look back and relive them all over and over again.

Journaling Tips

- **Write about your anticipation.** What are you looking forward to most and least before you go.

- **Your packing list.** List the items you need to pack/still need to get.

- **List the events of each travel day.** Write a simple list of the events of the day/expectations.

- **Record your travel time.** What time did you leave for the trip?

- **Record the costs.** Record how much you paid for your travel activities, lodging, transportation, and souvenirs.

- **Write about things you wished you could bring home.** Were there souvenirs you couldn't afford or were too big? What did you buy? How much did your purchases cost?

- **List your regrets.** Did you pack too many clothes? Do you wish you'd brought a backup camera and extra batteries?

- **List everything you lost during the trip.** Did you have to replace anything? Was anything stolen?

- **Record what/who you missed most during the trip.** Was it hard to be away from home?

- **Write about your expectations.** What were they before and after. How was it different than you expected?

- **Save the details you planned before you left.** What did you plan before? Transportation, hotels/B&B's, routes.

- **List everything you're thankful for.** Challenge yourself with how many things you can write each day.

- **Write advice you were given before you left.** How was the advice helpful?

- Record the high/low temperature of each day.
  What was the best and worst parts of the day?
- List unusual things: songs, movies, books, animals.
  What was different about them.
- Document your interaction with local people.
  Could you understand them? Did you ask for directions? Any
  unfamiliar languages? What did you hear people talking about?
- List what you missed. If you were to go back, what would
  you do differently next time?
- Document a typical day. When did you wake up, eat
  breakfast. How did you travel? How much did you spend? (etc.)
- List any major news events that happened during
  your trip. Where were you when those events happened?
  Did any world events affect your travels?
- Record the weather. If you write daily, make a small note
  at the top of each page about the day's weather.
- Record your feelings. How did the trip make you feel?
  Would you do it again?
- List unusual words. Write common words with different
  meanings. (For example, a car's trunk verses UK's boot.)
- Document your re-entry into the USA.
- Record your recommendations. If someone else
  were making the same trip, what would you recommend:
  restaurants, museums, tours, etc.

Add your own photos. Relive the memories again and again.

Enjoy the journey!

Twenty years from now
you will be more disappointed
by the things you didn't do
than by the ones you did do.
So... Explore.

Dream.

Discover.

MARK TWAIN

TRAVEL TIP: *Choose Your Clothing Wisely*

Even though you can't take your favorite wardrobe, you can still look fabulous. Choose clothing that can go with everything else that you are taking, like a white button-down shirt.

LAYERS: London weather changes quickly. Pack one or two heavy shirts only, and layers to go underneath. And remember, what you choose to wear will be seen in your videos and pictures for years.

The Coca-Cola London Eye
Riverside Building, County Hall
Westminster Bridge Road
London
SE1 7PB
www.londoneye.com

FREE
HOTSPOTS

Trafalgar Square
Downing Street
Big Ben
National Gallery
British Museum
Houses of Parliament
Westminster Bridge
Westminster Abbey
Buckingham Palace
Tate Modern
Greenwich Park
East London Street Art
Borough Market
Museum of London
Kensington Gardens
Queen's House
National Portrait Gallery
Natural History Museum
Victoria & Albert Museum
Sky Garden
St Paul's Church
Portobello Road Market
Science Museum
Sir John Soane's Museum
Temple Church
Wallace Collection

WINDPROOF TRAVEL UMBRELLA

It will rain. I recommend the Bodyguard Travel Umbrella.
From light drizzles to hardy rains, this compact,
wind-resistant umbrella will meet most of your needs.

All journeys
have secret destinations
of which the traveler

is unaware.

MARTIN BUBER

FREE ADVICE

1. Don't try to see it all.

2. Keep an eye on your drink tab.

3. Don't skip Camden Market.

4. Skip Buckingham Palace.
   It's a neat place, but not really worth a prolonged visit.

5. Don't skip out on the countryside.

6. Don't eat British food.
   The imported cuisine of London should not be missed.

7. You don't have to bring up the queen.

8. Don't stop on sidewalks.

9. Don't skip the tube, but don't forget to walk around either.

10. Don't forget the pub.
    The city is known for its distinct approach to brewing.

11. Don't eat or shop Chains.
    London has so many amazing food and shopping options that you're doing yourself a disservice.

Add your own

_____

_____

_____

_____

_____

_____

_____

_____

TRAVEL TIP: *Three Pairs of Shoes ONLY*
Pick one pair of "dressy" shoes, for an evening out.
One pair that will be comfortable on the airplane.
Your final pair should be what you plan to walk around in.
Keep this in mind when making clothing choices.

BUY AN OYSTER CARD

Valid not only on the underground, but also for the red double decker buses and even regional trains. You will save money — Oyster Cards have a daily maximum of £8.50 ($12) meaning you can visit all the sites in one day for a relatively good price.

He who would travel

happily

must travel light.

ANTOINE de SAINT-EXUPÉRY

Near Amesbury, Wiltshire
SP4 7DE
UK
Call: +44 0370 333 1181
www.english-heritage.org.uk

TRAVEL TIP: Make Lists

No matter where you are going, make a list of EVERYTHING you
are going to need from a toothbrush to socks. Make a list for each
day you will be away, including everything you will need to wear.
Once your list is made you are ready to select a suitcase.

For my part,
I travel not to go anywhere,
but to go.
I travel for travel's sake.
The great affair is to move.

ROBERT LOUIS STEVENSON

FACTS | Big Ben

The bell itself is officially called the "Great Bell," but gets its nickname from Sir Benjamin Hall, who became the first Commissioner of Public Works in 1855 and oversaw the later stages of the rebuilding of the Houses of Parliament. The previous Palace of Westminster had burned down as a result of the Great Fire of 1834. The Great Bell was cast in 1858 and has Sir Hall's name inscribed upon it. The "big" part comes from the fact that the bell weighs 16 tons and is about 7 feet tall.

TRAVEL TIP: *Take the Smallest Suitcase Possible*

Do your best to get all your things into one suitcase — and you shouldn't have to sit on it to close it. Repack trying to conserve space. You are going to have to make your way through airports, and throughout your journey, if you can't carry it, you've packed too much!

HAND TOWEL & EXTRA SHIRT

There is nothing worse than being wet in a cool breeze.
Carrying a small towel in your backpack will allow you to get
somewhat dry before you change into your extra shirt.

Do not follow
where the path may lead.
Go instead
where there is no path
and leave a trail.

RALPH WALDO EMERSON

Houses of Parliament
Westminster
London
SWIA 0AA
www.parliament.uk/visit

TRAVEL TIP: *Pack a Souvenir Bag*

Pack a collapsible bag that goes in our suitcase on your way
to England. As you buy souvenirs, put them in the bag. When it is
time to go home, carry the bag on the plane with you. You won't
need a bigger suitcase, and you are assured your souvenirs are
not crushed in your luggage.

Traveling—
it leaves you speechless,
then turns you into
a storyteller.

IBN BATTUTA

FACTS | Tower Bridge

The Tower Bridge is a combined bascule and suspension bridge in London
built between 1886 and 1894. The bridge crosses the River Thames close
to the Tower of London and has become an iconic symbol of London.
Because of this, Tower Bridge is sometimes confused with London Bridge,
situated about a half mile upstream. Tower Bridge is one of five London
bridges now owned and maintained by the Bridge House Estates, a
charitable trust overseen by the City of London Corporation. It is the only
one of the Trust's bridges not to connect the City of London directly to
the Southwark bank, as its northern landfall is in Tower Hamlets.

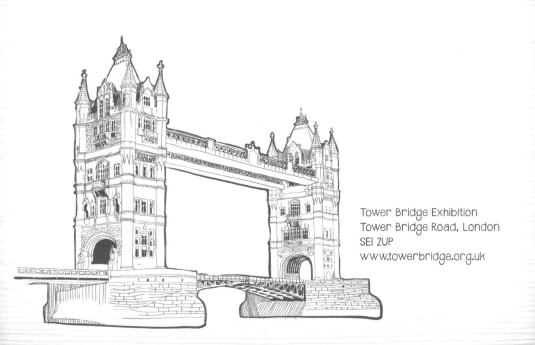

Tower Bridge Exhibition
Tower Bridge Road, London
SEI 2UP
www.towerbridge.org.uk

TRAVEL TIP: Take a Carry-on Bag

In case your suitcase disappears, this is your backup until it arrives.
A toothbrush and a change of clothes will get you comfortably
through a day or two. But make sure you pack only what you
would absolutely need.

A good traveler
has no fixed plans,
and is not intent
on arriving.

LAO TZU

FACTS | The Queen's Guard

The Queen's Guard and Queen's Life Guard (called King's
Guard and King's Life Guard when the reigning monarch
is male) are the names given to contingents of infantry
and cavalry soldiers charged with guarding the official
royal residences in the United Kingdom. The British Army
has regiments of both Horse Guards and Foot Guards
predating the English Restoration (1660), and since the reign
of King Charles II these regiments have been responsible
for guarding the Sovereign's palaces. They are not purely
ceremonial, despite tourist perceptions to the contrary.
The Queen's Guards are fully operational soldiers.

TRAVEL TIP: *Mix Up Your Suitcases*

If you are traveling with a spouse or close friend, put some
of your clothing in their luggage and vice-versa. If one suitcase is lost,
you are both sure to have at least some of your clothing.

We travel
not to escape life,
but for life
not to escape us.

ANONYMOUS

PHOTOGRAPH YOUR CONTENTS

Just in case the unthinkable happens, you have a record of what you have brought with you and can be identified quickly and effectively. Plus, you'll discover what you've left behind.

TRAVEL TIP: Keep Certain Things with You

All electronics, such as cameras and laptops, should never be packed

in your luggage! Make sure you have them in your carry-on bag.

And, ladies, always keep your jewelry with you.

Life is either
a daring adventure
or nothing.

HELEN KELLER

FACTS | Red Telephone Box

The red public telephone kiosk was designed by Sir Giles Gilbert Scott.
The color red was chosen to make them easy to spot. From 1926 onwards,
the fascias of the kiosks were emblazoned with a prominent crown,
representing the British government. The red phone box is often seen
as a British cultural icon throughout the world. In 2006 the K2 telephone
box was voted one of Britain's top 10 design icons, along with the AEC
Routemaster bus. The paint color used most widely today is known as
"currant red," slightly brighter than the red on the K8 model. So if you
notice a kiosk that is a bit darker red, it is most likely from before 1968.

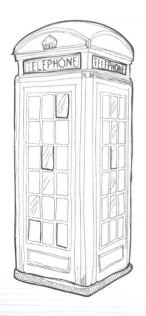

TRAVEL TIP: Make Copies of Passport & Birth Certificate

Actual passport should be carried with you while traveling via air,
and stash a paper copy of both documents somewhere in your luggage.
If your passport gets lost or stolen, you would need these documents.

Exploring the unexplored
is the most
adventurous part
of a traveler's life!

ANONYMOUS

BRING AN EMPTY WATER BOTTLE

Empty liquid containers will pass airport inspection.
Metal is a better option than plastic—it keeps liquids colder
longer and you will be less prone to leaving it on a bench.

TRAVEL TIP: *Check What You Can & Cannot Pack*

All countries have restrictions on what you can bring into that country.
You cannot bring certain foods, bottled water, certain cosmetics in a carry-on.
If you are unsure, check ahead with the airline you will be flying with.

Better to see
something once
than to hear about it
a thousand times.

ASIAN PROVERB

MAKE SOME ICE

If you have access to a freezer, fill you water bottle at least one-third full and freeze it overnight. In the morning, top off the bottle with water and it will stay cold most of the day.

TRAVEL TIP: *Plug Adapters*

Be sure to pack plug adapters for your gadgets (iPhone, etc.), as American
style plugs don't work in UK plug outlets. You can pick up plug adapters cheap.
In most cases, you will not need a voltage converter. Most American
electronics can be used in the UK with a simple plug adapter.

The man who goes alone
can start today;
but he who travels with another
must wait till that other
is ready.

HENRY DAVID THOREAU

MINI FIRST AID KIT & HAND TOWEL

A mini kit will cover minor scrapes and cuts that might occur.
Band-Aids, gauze pads, and small roll of tape in a small baggie.
It needs to fit in your backpack along with a small towel.

FACTS | England's Tea

Since the eighteenth century, the United Kingdom has
been one of the world's greatest tea consumers, with
an average annual per capita tea supply of 4.18 lbs. The
British Empire was instrumental in spreading tea from
China to India; British interests controlled tea production
in the subcontinent. Tea, which was an upper-class
drink in mainland Europe, became the infusion of every
social class in Great Britain throughout the course of
the eighteenth century and has remained so. Tea is a
prominent feature of British culture and society.

Once a year,

go some place

you've never been before.

My Travel Journal: London

© 2018 KPT Publishing, LLC
Written by D. A. Michaels

Published by KPT Publishing
Minneapolis, Minnesota 55406
www.KPTPublishing.com

ISBN 978-1-944833-50-3

Designed by AbelerDesign.com

First printing December 2018

10 9 8 7 6 5 4 3 2 1

Printed in the United States of America